Come, walk with me in mud

First published in 2025 by Libri Publishing

Copyright © Sushma Sharma

The right of Sushma Sharma to be identified as the author of this work has been asserted in accordance with the Copyright, Designs and Patents Act, 1988.

ISBN: 978-1-911451-38-9

All rights reserved. No part of this publication may be reproduced, stored in any retrieval system or transmitted in any form or by any means, electronic, mechanical, photocopying, recording or otherwise, without the prior written permission of the copyright holder for which application should be addressed in the first instance to the publishers. No liability shall be attached to the author, the copyright holder or the publishers for loss or damage of any nature suffered as a result of reliance on the reproduction of any of the contents of this publication or any errors or omissions in its contents.

A CIP catalogue record for this book is available from The British Library

Cover and Design by Carnegie Book Production
Cover image © Ajay Noronha

Libri Publishing
Brunel House
Volunteer Way
Faringdon
Oxfordshire
SN7 7YR

Tel: +44 (0)845 873 3837

www.libripublishing.co.uk

# Come, walk with me in mud

SUSHMA SHARMA

*This book is dedicated to my parents, and to all the participants who became my partners in learning.*

# ENDORSEMENTS FOR *COME, WALK WITH ME IN MUD*

"For years Sushma Sharma has been sharing her learnings and her wisdom in brief posts online. Now at last we have a collection in print of some of the best of what Sush Says!"

**Walt Hopkins, author, Member Emeritus of the NTL Institute, and founder of Castle Consultants International**

"Walking with Sushma in mud is an experience to savour. Unlike a conventional book, I didn't read it from cover to cover. I just opened a page randomly and another one and yet another one. Each page held an invitation to explore, a new door opening, a new perspective and also brought new questions for those that I thought I already had an answer. While the content on each page was different and the way of writing too, Sushma was there in each page with her flow."

**Sankarasubramanyan Ramamoorthy, author, OD Practitioner**

Life is beautifully messy. *Come, walk with me in mud* is an invitation to embrace imperfection and rediscover joy. Through poetic reflections, Sushma Sharma explores trust, vulnerability, and the courage to live authentically. Step into the mud, you may uncover wholeness, connection, and the freedom to truly be."

**Dr. Mosongo Moukwa, President, Hathaway Advanced Materials Inc.**

"This book feels like a gentle, yet powerful exhale – its words arriving in an unfiltered rush...alive in a way that compels our attention. Rather than forcing order into her prose, the author gathers these reflective moments into a vibrant kaleidoscope of colors and textures, offering them to the reader as a truly heartfelt gift. *Come, walk with me in mud* is an invitation to pause, to breathe, and to feel the beauty of what happens when our thoughts are allowed to simply be."

**Sukari Pinnock Fitt, MSOD, PCC, OD Scholar Practitioner**

"Sushma Sharma is an Iconic OD professional, teacher, friend, mentor and a voice from the deepest recesses of the heart. Her work, *Come, walk with me in mud*, is a compelling read of the inner workings of an insightful mind. Life is chaotic, that's the fun part, and perhaps walking in the mud with Sushma, some of the mud will stick to you. And you may wonder, am I that too? Then in Sushma's impish way, the book would have served its purpose."

**Shah Nawaz Ahmad, Nuclear Professional**

# CONTENTS

| | | |
|---|---|---|
| ACKNOWLEDGEMENTS | | IX |
| FOREWORD | | XI |
| INTRODUCTION | | 1 |
| 1 | A TRIP OF A LIFETIME | 3 |
| 2 | HAPPY INSPIRING MOMENTS | 5 |
| 3 | WE NEED TO LIVE FEMININE VALUES EVERY DAY | 6 |
| 4 | WHAT'S ALIVE IN YOU? | 7 |
| 5 | TRUST | 8 |
| 6 | HAPPY HUNTING YOU | 10 |
| 7 | A RAINBOW OF COLOURS | 12 |
| 8 | LEADING OTHERS | 14 |
| 9 | FACILITATION IS AN ART | 15 |
| 10 | FEELINGS | 17 |
| 11 | WHAT IS DIVERSITY REALLY? | 18 |

| | | |
|---|---|---|
| 12 | BUTTERFLIES IN THE STOMACH | 20 |
| 13 | YOU WILL FAIL! | 22 |
| 14 | EACH DAY IS A NEW BIRTH | 24 |
| 15 | APPROVE OF YOURSELF | 25 |
| 16 | LIKE THE SUDDEN RAINBOW | 27 |
| 17 | RECIPE FOR COACHING | 28 |
| 18 | ROMANCE AND US | 30 |
| 19 | LEADERS ARE MADE OF THESE | 31 |
| 20 | DECONSTRUCT SELF AND RE-EMERGE FROM THE ASHES | 32 |
| 21 | OUR DESIRE | 34 |
| 22 | EMPOWER PEOPLE AND MAKE THEM REFLECT | 35 |
| 23 | IT'S LIKE A ROSE | 36 |
| 24 | DO I REALLY MATTER? | 38 |
| 25 | BE YOUR OWN MIDWIFE | 39 |
| 26 | THE TEARS FLOWED LIKE A RIVER | 40 |
| 27 | BE A GOOD GIRL OR A GOOD BOY | 42 |
| 28 | WE ARE SCARED OF OUR OWN LIGHT | 44 |
| 29 | ENJOY THE MOMENT FULLY WITH ABANDON | 46 |
| 30 | THE COURAGE TO BE DISLIKED | 48 |

| | | |
|---|---|---|
| 31 | LET'S BECOME STRANGERS AGAIN | 50 |
| 32 | THE ANSWER IS BLOWING IN THE WIND | 51 |
| 33 | LIKE A BUTCHER WE START FRAGMENTING OURSELVES | 53 |
| 34 | MEMORIES FLOOD MY BEING | 55 |
| 35 | NURTURE THE CHILD IN YOU | 56 |
| 36 | IT IS SO BLOODY SUBTLE! | 58 |
| 37 | NOT ENOUGH | 60 |
| 38 | LOVE LIKE THERE IS NO TOMORROW | 62 |
| 39 | THAT WAS WRITTEN IN ONE BREATH! | 63 |
| 40 | WHAT AM I GIVING BIRTH TO IN THE MOMENT? | 65 |
| 41 | JUST TRY IT | 66 |
| 42 | I AM PICKING UP THE SMALL CHANGES | 68 |
| 43 | POWER IS A DYNAMIC PROCESS | 70 |
| 44 | WHERE ARE WE HEADED? | 72 |
| 45 | DISCOVERING NEW NOTES | 74 |
| 46 | LIKE BEGGARS WE KEEP STANDING | 75 |
| 47 | VOLUNTARISM AS A VALUE | 77 |
| 48 | IT IS TIME TO CLAIM OUR REAL POWER | 79 |

| | |
|---|---|
| 49 HAPPY JOURNEY | 81 |
| 50 DISCOVERY OF SELF | 83 |
| 51 FEELINGS | 85 |
| 52 LIFE WILL EXPAND | 87 |
| 53 INTERPERSONAL WETLANDS | 88 |
| 54 A QUESTION OF QUESTIONS | 91 |
| 55 CONNECTING IS A DEEP PROCESS | 95 |
| 56 HAPPY LEARNING | 98 |
| 57 FEARS ARE A PART OF LIFE | 100 |
| 58 SOME FOOD FOR THOUGHT | 102 |
| 59 BE THE FLOWING RIVER THAT BRINGS CALM | 104 |
| 60 CREATING NEW POSSIBILITIES | 105 |
| 61 A MIRACLE IS ON ITS WAY | 107 |
| 62 A FOUR-LETTER WORD | 109 |
| 63 WHAT THE HELL ARE FEELINGS? | 110 |
| 64 IT JUST CUT MY HEART INTO PIECES | 113 |
| 65 THE LEADER IS READY TO FLOW | 115 |
| ABOUT THE AUTHOR | 117 |

# ACKNOWLEDGEMENTS

My heart is overflowing with love and joy as I think about the word 'acknowledgements'. Had it not been for my friend Walt Hopkins this idea of a book would not have occurred to me. His relentless faith in me and my writing has given birth to this book. He acted as the midwife, encouraging, empathising, chiding – and by just being there. My gratitude also goes to Ajay Noronha, who spent days and nights editing and giving it a shape with his loving heart. I have felt overwhelmed by the love and trust shown to me by so many others like Abhishek Thakore, Rhea D'Souza and Shah Nawaz Ahmad.

Last words of my joy are for the presence and silent cajoling by my life partner Raji Sharma, Surabhi Sharma, George Jose and my granddaughter Sanah George. My cup of joy is very heady.

Thanks to the many people who have liked and resonated with these pieces. I feel so expanded.

# FOREWORD

More than 25 years ago, I met Sushma when Charlie Seashore, then president of NTL, introduced her to a group of us. With great enthusiasm he shared that Sushma was the President of NTL's sister organization, ISABS, she had coached hundreds of CEOs, she was a poet – on and on he went. I started to feel embarrassed, wondering if it was a bit much, and still he continued. Sushma sat there, smiling, nodding with each new accolade. When he finally stopped, she added, "And Charlie, there is one more thing – I am very sensual." We all laughed, and that was the first time I fell in love with Sushma – followed by many more.

Over the years we discovered that we are soul sisters, deeply bonded despite the distance. Our intimacy has carried us through laughter, loss, and countless adventures. We've traveled to so many places together – sometimes with a plan, more often letting the adventure unfold. Whether kayaking down a river or improvising an activity in a workshop, Sushma leans toward the wild edge. She speaks poetry in everyday conversations, catching me off guard with a mischievous grin, a sideways question, or a sudden detour that takes us into unknown territory.

Sushma and I have walked down winding country roads, the crowded streets of Mumbai, gardens in full bloom, and we've shared our inner worlds where laughter and grief sit side by side. She has a way of inviting the messiness in, and reading her poetry feels like being by her side – unguarded, alive, full of sudden turns that lead us into long silences or wanting to catch our breath. Her words are like wildflowers gathered and gifted again in the next encounter.

What I treasure most about Sushma is how she integrates wisdom and play, tears and laughter, vulnerability and leadership. Again and again, she invites us into the space where it's real and full of aliveness. *Come, walk with me in mud* is her gift, and like all her gifts, it carries her extraordinary loving presence: mischievous, tender, daring, and wickedly funny as she finds beauty in every step.

**Martha Lasley, Partner at Authentic Communication Group**

# INTRODUCTION

I have travelled around the world quite often, for work and for pleasure. Each new space fills me with curiosity. Different cultures raise my awareness to deeper reflection. I felt stimulated and energised, so that each day I sat down to capture what was bubbling inside me. Without much ado the words kept rushing out like people jumping out of a crowded local train. I didn't have time to arrange them it was so random. I just stepped aside and let them come like a flood, soaking me totally.

I didn't look forward to making logical connections but kept collecting them like one picks up wild flowers. The vibrant colours hook me. So I have tried to make bouquet of these leaves and flowers and am offering it as a gift.

Stay with the randomness and spontaneity of it; read just one page at a time or read the whole book. My hope is that it will resonate with you and stir you to reflection.

Shy Foliage

A smile here, a smile there
Hesitant, shy looks
Hands clasping and unclasping
Aware yet unaware
Like the buds on the trees
Yearnings in the quiver of their lips
Just like deer running away
Wanting to speak
Not having the language
But the heart speaking volumes
Hugs saying the word love
The dance conveying inner yearnings
Whoever willing to be touched by that!

Happy reading.

Sush Says
Mumbai, March 2024

# 1

# A TRIP OF A LIFETIME

It was a trip of a lifetime. Not just discovering Hampi but also discovering self. Taking this decision to go just because I wanted to was another journey. I had no desire to prove anything but just to soak. Whatever was enticing to us, we spent more time there. No hurry, no need to see everything – the main purpose was to explore, and that included us as people too. Talking to strangers, watching monkeys play or the experience of a boat ride or watching Bharatnatyam and dhols being played by four spunky people filled us, all our senses being satisfied. It was a sensuous experience. The smells, flowers, awesome trees and those boulders almost like a painting. The etchings on those stones, water bodies and spirituality. How people wore their best attire to visit these temples and take a dip in the sacred river.

I noticed the love the boatman had for his craft and how he showed off his skill. The delight in his whole being when he held binoculars in his hands. His wonder at this first-time experience was infectious.

The endless discussions, sharing memories from days gone by, a time to be just silent, asking uncanny questions about politics, culture, growth, dilemmas and love. Food for thought and body.

I could go on and on. Hampi is to be savoured, to be marvelled at and to be experienced fully with no hurry. I am so glad that I listened to my calling. The whole universe conspired to make it happen.

# 2

# HAPPY INSPIRING MOMENTS

How does one choose a theme or a topic? It's not an intellectual exercise. If it is, then it's sterile, it doesn't evoke much.

I have to sense, to feel, it emerges from within.
Like a surprise it takes you by the gut.
It has the right ingredients of being evocative and provocative.
It's almost an inspired state of being where a muse appears and catches hold of you, then you check with a few others.
In the first instance, if their eyes light up, then you got it.
If each and every person reacts almost in that way –
a wide smile, glowing eyes –
that means you caught the right nerve,
it's not forced or artificial,
it's real, natural labour pains, no caesarean operation,
the baby comes out howling leaving you all bloody and sweaty.

# 3

# WE NEED TO LIVE FEMININE VALUES EVERY DAY

Celebrating woman's day is different. Like you celebrate Diwali. It's true that we need to live feminine values every day. It's a kind of a reminder to men and women of who we are. We need not propagate virtues of compromise and dependence. Organisations that ritualistically celebrate, yet are not inclusive or are obsessively masculine need to take cognisance of this issue. The hope is that they will slowly wake up till it becomes part of them.

The women need to become more self-aware and tap into their own essence and dreams. It will take a hell of a time for culture and societies to change. One can already see women's power and leadership emerging during recent protests. Hopefully the day is not far when women will empower themselves even more and men will equally use their feminine qualities.

# 4

# WHAT'S ALIVE IN YOU?

Diversity as a theme is an important piece to learn, especially as a leader. Diversity is not only of gender but of language, education, talents, colour, caste, social identities, sexuality, religion, nationality, region, age, ability, styles of dressing and communication, to name but a few. All the biases, hidden or visible, that we carry and are unconscious of. Apart from that, there is so much to us as a person. All the parts I acknowledge and own, the parts I disown.

The only path to understand this is through awareness, curiosity and vulnerability.

The first step is awareness of what I include and exclude. Some lingering thoughts in my heart.

To be continued after I hear your comments and stories...

# 5

# TRUST

Trust needs openness
And openness means
Courage
To be fully me.
Share openly but with sensitivity
To listen fully
Letting the other person or group influence you.
Taking risks is fundamental to trust.
Ambiguity needs trust in self and others to go with the flow.
Imagine jumping into water.
The joy of being in water is the consequence of taking a risk.
Everything in life is a risk.
The biggest risk we take is to get married.
Who knows the future?
Yet we stir out.

Testing
Reaching out
Understanding
Surprise
Together

# 6

# HAPPY HUNTING YOU

How many times we think of ourselves as parts. Some parts we acknowledge and accept and some parts are lost and forgotten in our to-do list. The whole idea of life is to discover, be curious and become whole again. We are very large and grand but have made a miniature of ourselves. We have shrunk our desires, wishes, dreams in search of perfection and control. We have created so many boundaries that our soul has become a prisoner.

We seem to have no time to imagine, dream and rest. I loved reading, somewhere creating that me time, doing nothing, just lying down, listening to music and letting my mind wander like Alice in Wonderland.

We speak to people about our restlessness and discomfort at being stuck in the same rut. Those people who are apparently concerned for us. They advise us: 'Just focus on what you are doing. Why do you want to listen to such nonsense in your head?' Don't go to such people, people who have marginalised many parts of themselves. Shape shifting happens when you take those tiny steps to free yourself and expand your limiting beliefs. Listen to the desires that you have without thinking about the end product. This need for perfect outcomes doesn't allow you to be vulnerable, to be curious like a child and to define a new identity. We are born to be very large and to keep searching and discovering our parts.

Let's not play three blind men and an elephant. Unless we see ourselves as a complete elephant we are miniaturising ourselves and are happy and content with our successes. Disruption means growth. If you feel discomfort or panic then you are bang on the right path.

Embrace the real you with fears, warts and many ugly things. No need to hide your light, it need not be like the headlights of a car in the dark yet it needs to be unabashedly owned and worn by you.

# 7

# A RAINBOW OF COLOURS

What is life? A rainbow of colours.
On a wet day, waves thrashing the edges of land and claiming their space...
Birds flying in the sky, a gentle smile that touches your heart when you are grieving...
A child being born each minute...
Birds clamouring their identity in the thick of humanity at dusk...
Children coming home in the evening...

The act of leading is not an activity or a to-do list. It is a process of flowering and spreading your wings. You have to fall in love with flying, your essence, your thoughts. Basically, who you are and who you are becoming are the roots of leadership.

What is being alive? An awareness of my sensuality, when all senses come together and a symphony is created. Of sounds of life, of more fragrances mystical and alluring, of tastes sprinkled with spices of life complete with tears and smiles, anxieties and vulnerabilities, fears and joys. When touch creates vibrations and flexibility, nuances of the touch bring my heart into my mouth. When feelings of love overwhelm me and I go blind as if falling from an edge. Like the excitement of a rollercoaster ride, the shrieking and screaming like a kid. When I tremble and shiver on seeing a beautiful painting or reading a poem.

Coaching is more of an art than a science. The recipe for good coaching is passion for people, flowing with the river, keeping yourself aside, adding a pinch of courage and stirring it with letting go. Sometimes this and that add to the flavour. Each time it has to be new ingredients. Tried and tested makes it stale.

# 8

# LEADING OTHERS

Leading others is a path strewn with possibilities and pitfalls. Being afraid of falling will make you depend on known devils, which is a sure route to falling in a big way. Exploring the unknown requires trust and adventure and being in touch with self in a big way.

Try the new.

Discovering self is a lifelong agenda. Each and every turn throws up surprises. A figure you can't recognise embracing new flavours is the only way.

# 9

# FACILITATION IS AN ART

It's a process of being one with your being and doing. The first part is really self and your awareness of self. What are your values, needs, wants, fears, anxieties, your challenges and edges, prejudices and biases? The acceptance of everything is the first building block. Use of self as an instrument of change. My anxieties are going to interfere with my facilitation. Patience and compassion are needed for the emergence to happen. It's difficult to watch the struggle of the group. We rush in to help. Because we have committed to some outcomes, takeaways. Now it becomes your baby. You really want them to learn instead of creating an environment that triggers people to learn. Just a nudge here and there. Being scared to confront is a big hurdle to deeper learning. Needing to be liked may divert you from the real purpose of the group.

Facilitation is not a magic potion that you carry, it is hard work. The work of keeping yourself in check and confronting your own shadow and demons. Transferring the leadership to participants, empowering them to move forward. It can be distressing and de-energising to wait and watch.

Only a plant knows when it needs to show up.

# 10

# FEELINGS

Why are feelings downgraded?
What is the history behind it? You are too emotional.
Nobody says your logic stinks.
What is the resistance to feelings?

Love, anger, jealousy, joy, affection, curiosity, sadness, fear and so on.
It seems to push the envelope somehow.
No wonder we are saddled with so many diseases.
Heart attack, stress, blood pressure, cancer, to name just a few.

What is the narrative in our mind?
Women are supposed to feel.
It's okay, they are an inferior lot anyways.
Men are supposed to be strong, and hence devoid of feelings.
What is the story?
What is the story we carry in our head and heart?
I have many answers created by logic.
But I am curious to explore more.

Are you?

# 11

# WHAT IS DIVERSITY REALLY?

Most of the time, we try to ape and conform for the sake of validation. Killing our unique quotient day by day. Marginalising our many parts while polishing a few for the world to see and admire. The first task is to know our parts and own up to them. Even the ones we have hidden in a closet away from the prying eyes of the world, just for the sake of approval. When will we grow up and accept those funny, interesting, bubbly, faulty, rusty parts? Those are the unpolished gems concealing your varied talents needing some sunshine.

Let's not try to teach people diversity and inclusion while we are guilty of marginalising the parts of us that enjoy getting drenched in the rain, dancing when no one is looking, enjoying a good book or writing poetry, even doing silly hobbies that give us life.

There is plentiful life in you and not only in your persona. Stay diverse and have the guts to be different.

'Being different can actually be advantageous if you learn to embrace it, not to mention the fact that it will spice up your life. It highlights your originality and authenticity, and makes you stand out in a world full of conformity.'

'The person who follows the crowd will usually go no further than the crowd. The person who walks alone is likely to find himself in places no one has ever seen before.' – Albert Einstein

# 12

# BUTTERFLIES IN THE STOMACH

Many people are familiar with the experience of stomach sensations – butterflies in the stomach, trembling, weakness and sweaty palms in response to a state of fear or excitement. These are the body's complex responses to a mental condition called excitement. It's exhilarating to feel excitement.

When the heart comes into the mouth and is almost ready to jump out. Such moments are etched in our heart. As fear takes control and our judgements are supervisors of our personality, we learn to become stoic, so much so that we forget even to laugh uncontrollably. Remember how as a young person we felt excited about everything, without a care in the world. Sometimes we jumped or even danced in the middle of a crowd...

As Wordsworth said:

My heart leaps up when I behold
A rainbow in the sky:
So was it when my life began;
So is it now I am a man;
So be it when I shall grow old,
Or let me die!

# 13

# YOU WILL FAIL!

Trust is the cornerstone of our existence. When we feel trusted from childhood, our confidence level is of a different nature.

'You will break this'; 'don't pick that up'; 'you will lose money'; 'you will get lost'; 'you don't know how to do that'; 'you are too young'; 'you can't carry this'; 'you will fail'. So many, in fact innumerable, such messages accost a child, an adolescent – and indeed adults. This kind of message leaves an indelible impression on our psyche. We grow up feeling inadequate and invalidated. On the other hand, too much validation robs us of our own understanding. Approval becomes an integral part of our growing up, which lasts till we die.

Trusting someone to do right is another ball game. 'You can do it'; 'just try slowly'; 'my god, how did you manage this?' Such messages create a different energy. When a leader trusts you, your judgement, your intentions, your values, the growth is simply a delight to see.

The need to control gives the message 'I don't trust you', whereas freedom has trust inherent in it. It creates spontaneity, creativity and the ability to take risks. Not trusting and distrusting have other dimensions.

I remember reading a book in Hindi, *Shekhar: Ek Jeevani*. The parents are discussing one of their children in the kitchen, the elder brother, who has been arrested for being a communist. He has refused to mention his father's name at the police station. The father says that he doesn't trust even Shekhar, who overhears this. Shekhar goes through a tremendous struggle. If his parents don't trust him, he thinks, what's the point of being with them? So he runs away from home, deeply wounded.

I have heard many such stories.

Trusting someone needs deep trust in self.

## 14

# EACH DAY IS A NEW BIRTH

Early morning drives are very magical, with the sun bursting forth from the chest of the sky, almost like childbirth, bringing joy and delight.

Each day is a new birth, bringing different kinds of identities. By afternoon it has grown young, with youthful arrogance, and by the evening it is like post-retirement, calm and romantic.

By night it dies, giving place to a beautiful night full of darkness, with the moon playing Cupid, and once again it's ready to deliver a new day.

# 15

# APPROVE OF YOURSELF

'A man cannot be comfortable without his own approval.'

If you don't approve of yourself, of your behaviour and actions, then you'll probably walk around most of the day with a sort of uncomfortable feeling. If, on the other hand, you approve of yourself then you tend to become relaxed and gain inner freedom to do more of what you really want.

This can, in a related way, be a big obstacle in personal growth. You may have all the right tools to grow in some way but you feel an inner resistance. You can't get there.

What you may be bumping into are success barriers. You are putting up barriers in your own mind of what you may or may not deserve. Or barriers that tell you what you are capable of. They might tell you that you aren't really the kind of person who could do this thing that you're attempting.

Or if you make some headway in the direction you

want to go, you may start to sabotage yourself, to keep yourself in a place that is familiar to you.

So you need to give yourself approval and allow yourself to be who you want to be. Don't look for approval from others, but from yourself. To dissolve that inner barrier or let go of that self-sabotaging tendency.

This is no easy task and it can take time.

# 16

# LIKE THE SUDDEN RAINBOW

I am most optimistic at the lowest of times and have been this way from childhood. I am almost never given to mistrust. This optimist in me creates a new canvas to paint upon. Going with the flow and dealing with emergent realities brings a plethora of options and creative ideas.

It is as if the sea starts parting, to give way to new thoughts. Very rarely, do I become anxious. Anxiety comes from premeditated outcomes. The lesser the chances of achieving an outcome, the more the anxiety. We fail to notice the new options life is throwing at us.

New colours, new textures and new ambience, and umpteen new options and outcomes like the sudden rainbow in the sky after heavy rains.

Let's go with the flow and learn to be curious and surprised.

# 17

# RECIPE FOR COACHING

One tablespoon full of enthusiasm
Two tablespoons full of trust
Three tablespoons full of love
One teaspoon full of challenge
A pinch of edginess
Finely cut curious questions
Half a bowl of humour
Laced with intuition
A glass full of listening.
Mix well and garnish with self-awareness.

Flirting with life
Opened a can of worms.
Mischief,
Romance,
Adventure,
Edgy, risky,
Teasing, saucy, sensuous,
Joyful stories poured out.

How conditioning blocks our free expression! That spontaneous response in the moment when you throw caution to the wind and jump. The stories led to a sense of positive energy and a feeling of freedom. We celebrated life and discovered ourselves once again. How to live and create such moments where the unknown guides us and the best of ourselves springs forth?

## 18

# ROMANCE AND US

In our mundane life we have forgotten to be romantic. Most romantic poetry is about nature and its mysterious ways. It is an adventure. Our life needs romance to be alive, both in work and in relationships. Aesthetics play a great role in romance. To see beauty in everything and everyone. A sense of curiosity lets you ask new and interesting questions.

# 19

# LEADERS ARE MADE OF THESE

Genuineness creates a container into which you can pour pure feelings, thoughts, real enquiry and an ability to take risk. Your presence creates the link. Like a river flowing into the ocean. Creating bonds beyond imagination. When your intentions and actions are congruent.

Leaders are made of these ingredients.

# 20

# DECONSTRUCT SELF AND RE-EMERGE FROM THE ASHES

To stay in the here and now is a tough proposition. Our mind plays tricks and constantly brings past memories to warn us, to hold us as prisoners of the past. We are not in touch with our experience of the moment. Even when we are in touch, there is a disbelief, a doubt, as the memories cast a big shadow on our experience. Safety is a paramount concern. Getting hurt is not an option.

I was watching a Thai serial, *I Need Romance*, in which the protagonist has grown up disconnected from her feelings. She has so much difficulty recognising her feelings and expressing her love. To utter the three words 'I love you' takes her forever, thus depriving herself of knowing who she really is.

Some fears dominate and we repeat our patterns of life. If my belief is that I am rejected, I continue to pick up similar data all the time and reject the data where I am accepted. Self-awareness is the key to this lock. That's the catch. We understand these patterns intellectually. Knowledge doesn't help us to break these patterns or change, for that matter. One has to continuously deconstruct self and re-emerge from the ashes, sculpting a new self, keeping our values intact.

The exploration can be exciting, as if you are meeting a stranger each time. Trusting self and others, and examining our belief systems, is a slippery path but well worth the effort.

## 21

# OUR DESIRE

Our desire to be perfect is a big trap.
'I am not enough. I always need to be better than.'

At first, we may think that trying to be 'perfect' is desirable.

Let's take a closer look.

Perfection suggests a state of flawlessness, without imperfections. Imagine looking at a rainbow and complaining that the colours weren't perfect. Ridiculous!?

We would also be ruining the splendour of the moment. And yet, that is exactly what we do each time we judge – ourselves and others.

## 22

# EMPOWER PEOPLE AND MAKE THEM REFLECT

Creating engagement is a tough process. How do you lead in a way that allows people to be engaged and to feel connection? Disengaging is very quick. Just in a moment we can withdraw and opt out emotionally. One of the ways to prevent this is to listen to each story and discover the life-giving forces within it.

This process can create space for trust and openness.

Noticing what's working is a huge skill. When you don't focus only on what's not working but more on what's working, being curious, asking questions in order to know, not for enquiry or interrogation. Using questions that empower people and make them reflect is a sure way for deep connection.

A culture that expands us rather than shrinking our boundaries, where we are not tip-toeing and being too cautious.

Maybe you will add more to it.

## 23

# IT'S LIKE A ROSE

The group is not empowered when you withdraw and withhold. That's a myth. You are still acting like a parent, witnessing their growth and believing that you have done your job. It's only when you become one of the cogs of the wheel that it moves evenly. Your comments are part of the process. No one is paying more attention to you than to the words of others. The ideas of each participant are being listened to and implemented. It's a beautiful sight to witness.

If the others expand because you are shrinking, that's not real. What is the need for shrinking, just to allow others to expand? It can be one of the stages of group life, but the truth is that a group comes alive with equal participation from all when a leader/facilitator is also expanding. The creativity flows from all and an idea is appreciated more than who said what.

It's like a rose. Each petal opening up and helping the rose to bloom fully.

Interdependence at its ultimate. It's a vast expanse with no boundaries.

I walked in the rain. I made some essential purchases, but the real purpose was to roam around with a mask on my face, feeling the rain kissing my dress and my arms, like a truant child. The glee of nobody knowing I was out on the road. The joy of flirting with the winds. Then I noticed a plant that had totally bloomed vibrant orange.

## 24

# DO I REALLY MATTER?

I matter and I listen to my feelings.
Do I really matter?

Does it matter if I matter?
How does it matter that I matter or don't?
How do I know whether I matter or not?

During these times we may find ourselves asking these very existential questions. Some of us might even be pondering about the futility of asking such questions. Yet we seem to need meaningful recognition and a sense of making meaningful impact. Is this what we call 'value'?

In these present times, what is 'valuable' – for ourselves, for our loved ones, for mankind and for our planet?

## 25

# BE YOUR OWN MIDWIFE

All that you are engaged in, preoccupied with, how does it nourish you, make you really happy? Do you look forward to waking up each morning with a spring in your feet? If it's just keeping you busy then what is it worth? You are slowly losing yourself, your life force, your essence.

Don't be a block to your own passion and purpose. If you are just busy and go on with life, day in and day out, is it really worth it? Somewhere lurking around is that part of you that's yearning to do something more meaningful. Get out of the way with your logic and practicality. Let it be born, what's really needing to get born.

Be your own midwife.

## 26

# THE TEARS FLOWED LIKE A RIVER

As the lab was on, at crucial times the birds would start their song; very often it was the koyal. She would go on creating music as if she sensed what was on in the lab. A tune for reflection or lightening the mood or adding to the chaos. At other times there were other birds with their chirping and music. There was a yearning whistle as people broke through their self-imposed conditioning. The tears flowed like a river unabashedly. Just as tears ended, a new tune was set in motion by the birds.

I felt as if a drama was unfolding against this background score. For the whole five days we had a free orchestra to match the mood of the stories. What a joy they added. I started to decipher the changes in the koyal's tunes in the morning, afternoon and evening. The lilting tunes were so pleasing to the heart and soul.

Joy lies in connecting with self. Like singing from gut level not just from the throat, and discovering new notes.

Despite all the odds, living one's truth is the answer.

Courage is to show up as who I am, rather than who I should be seen as.

# 27

# BE A GOOD GIRL OR A GOOD BOY

Once upon a time, as all stories start, there lived a prince and a princess. Joyful and beautiful. Gleefully they played, joyfully they clapped, clowned about. Then gloom fell on their joyful souls. As a tyrant took over their lives. Control, rules and perfection were the new religion. Conform or get out. If you want to be loved and given all the favours then listen. Be a good girl or a good boy. The spell was cast. Discipline is to be lived by. Swallow your tears and eat up your sighs. What is spontaneity? It is the fodder of unruly children.

Slowly your brain was washed with so-called love and conditions. You became a shadow of your old self. Sing, dance, play, study with a goal in mind and an outcome. The rest is all rubbish. I have very high expectations of you. Fulfil my dreams for you. We gave you birth and toiled to have you standing on your own two feet. Never forget what we have done for you.

Get married and give us grandchildren. It's your duty to listen to us. You dare to stand up and confront us! Is this the tradition we have brought you up in? If today you are anything, it's all because of our struggles, love and the joys we deprived ourselves of.

The story ends on a bright note with success and all the expectations fulfilled, the debts to the parents being paid daily. They feel like the Pathan's debts: the interest is ever increasing.

You locked away your childhood, your feelings, your dreams, your heartbeats. You don't know anymore how to laugh, how to run joyfully. This life is all about responsibilities.

Happy ending! The prince and princess lived happily ever after.

# 28

# WE ARE SCARED OF OUR OWN LIGHT

Concealing and hiding is the process for many of us. Our secret desires, our passion, our joys, sadness, anger, tears and, above all, love.

We master the art of concealing to perfection with a drop-dead expression, fake smiles and joyful exuberance. How are you feeling? I am fine. You know what 'fine' stands for: f**ked up, insecure, neurotic, emotional. Whenever somebody tells me I am fine, I look for telltale signs of all this. In New York, I observed how people walking on the streets will see you and put on this false smile. It's amazing to witness this phenomenon.

Almost steeling ourselves against our vulnerability. Who suffers most from this hiding? We ourselves. People do it after experiencing neglect, insensitivity, being misunderstood. They get sympathy or advice cloaked under so-called concern.

It's not a safe place, this world of ours with its teeming millions. So what's the point? Let me deal with it in my own way. I don't need anyone. We choose a path fraught with less pain, without realising how much of ourselves we are shutting down. Wearing a mask all the time, not only when a pandemic hits us.

What are we hiding? It is not just our feelings and thoughts; we are scared of our own light and power. We want to shine but don't want to shine. We deprive ourselves of the possibility of discovery, curiosity and adventures, getting stuck in the black hole of our make-believe world. We are hiding our beauty, which is unique. The pity is that we don't believe this. So many assumptions and conclusions. It is a huge burden to carry on our tiny shoulders.

What's at stake here? You are investing in a bad share. There is good news and bad news. The good news is that you can be safe in that prison; the bad news is that you are missing out on life, fun and frolic.

# 29

# ENJOY THE MOMENT FULLY WITH ABANDON

Anxiety is a big killer. Worry about what may happen. Fear of the unknown expresses itself in so many ways. Our first thought goes to what can go wrong. It's a great burden to carry all our lives. It seems like an excuse not to enjoy the moment fully with abandon.

Many of us grow up with such conditioning as *nazar lag jayegi*, an evil eye that will cast a shadow. I remember as a young girl, whenever my sister and I would go out and have a rollicking time, invariably it would be spoilt by coming home to a resounding scolding. Then we manufactured a strategy: whenever we enjoyed ourselves, sitting in an autorickshaw, we would start feeling sad or down. Lo and behold, returning home would be peaceful! Thankfully, we didn't carry this through our lives.

What does worrying achieve, really? What's the reason behind not enjoying the moment? With our anxiety we become a killjoy for others too. It's another way of controlling people. Exercising our power in negative ways. Instead of accepting our vulnerability and dealing with it, we become anxious not about real stuff but future probabilities.

This blocks us from living to our full potential, spreading those wings. What will happen is going to happen any which way. You can't stop it. You might as well turn that corner and discover something new. Give a push to your free spirit, that childlike curiosity that's lurking behind. Sing that song that you never dared to sing, sing out of tune, dance with two left feet and let the world worry.

Que sera, sera
Whatever will be, will be
The future's not ours to see.

# 30

# THE COURAGE TO BE DISLIKED

Where do you get your energy from? The right question to explore would be how, when and where do you lose your energy every day?

There are many conversations that are so depleting. We hate them yet we continue to entertain them. Ignoring the ring of the phone doesn't help, as such people are persistent. What stops us from being upfront. We are hiding under layers of lies. Trying to have a persona which is endearing. What's the price we are paying? Have you ever thought about it? The courage to be disliked is the key.

Those millions of moments we have given up to be seen as responsible and courteous. While our heart burnt in protest. We don't even listen to our body sensations that have a new story to tell. Breathlessness, faster heartbeat, indigestion, headache and you name it, we have it. We spend enormous amounts of time, money and energy on medication to find a cure.

We take up millions of tasks to keep up the image of perfection till exhaustion hits us. There is no energy coming back to you. You are only giving and giving, helping others, taking care of everyone, except yourself. Nobody even stops to stand and stare. You are the pillar of strength everyone leans on. It's joyful to some extent but then the petrol runs out, and you can't move anymore.

Those hierarchical leaders with a mule mindset and gender biases can be tiring, day in and day out. Unless we name it openly and create conversations which are real and authentic, we can go on seething with anger and suppressed rage. No amount of diversity-and-inclusion sessions help. That's where the energy drains the most. We feed on fear and fear feeds on us. That's the end of the story. My job, my organisation, my relationships, my friendships, my siblings, my parents and finally my children. We thrive on fake stuff.

How do I show up? What does my presence bring? Am I heard and do I make myself visible? What do I notice about myself? Why and what for? Half of your life is over; you might as well take a jump and leap into the universe with new energy.

## 31

# LET'S BECOME STRANGERS AGAIN

In order to be friends with myself I need to forget who I am or was. I have to face myself as a stranger once again with no fear, shame or hesitation. I need to get a clear view of myself, blemishes and all. It is still a pretty picture with dimples, curious eyes and a smile playing mischievously.

Maybe I will discover many things afresh, all that I had discarded. Surprisingly, it looks pretty and inviting. Maybe I will start using it again. There was my assertiveness lying alone. I hugged it and wore it after a long time. Oh look at the child's likeness, in a corner sulking. Come on, let's go and play in the garden.

All this will happen if we are ready to be strangers again.

# 32

# THE ANSWER IS BLOWING IN THE WIND

Most of us tend to shrink when we make a mistake or find we having unknowingly offended someone. It puts us on the back foot. Not wanting to hurt anyone, our quick reaction is to become extra conscious. To suppress ourselves when faced with strangers or a new culture. To make ourselves invisible, almost. This guilty feeling makes us unnatural, almost bound in a prison, not even breathing fully just in case you hurt someone again.

The answer is blowing in the wind. We can't always be walking on eggshells. This feeling just means you've become more sensitive, and that's how you expand your energy and embrace new cultures. Each step takes you closer to becoming closer to people. As you expand with each breath you take, your learning and joy increases.

There is a big distinction between sensitively listening and being cautious. Listening makes you embrace your being, and in addition this embraces others in a new conversation.

Try it to know the difference!

## 33

# LIKE A BUTCHER WE START FRAGMENTING OURSELVES

Uncertainty is a huge disrupter. All our lives we strive to be certain, aiming for predictability, learning about planning goals and structures. Discipline is taught from childhood, to tame our roving selves. Boundaries are taught to keep track of everything, be it our movements, friends, love, religion, sexual orientation and much more. People can't control our thoughts, yet attempts are made to brainwash us. Some of us survive this attack on our natural, spontaneous self, yet others fall by the wayside.

Brick by brick our being is assaulted.

There is order in disorder and chaos in order. Life brings us to that spot where everything is uncertain and unpredictable. Now we are being asked to develop this as a competency. Thrive in ambiguity. The irony of it all is that a baby naturally knows how to swim, yet we are scared to let go. You put a baby in water even at two months old and it starts swimming like a champ. But our need to create templates to shape the world kills us emotionally, intellectually and even physically, to some extent.

Nowadays, we are talking about organic growth after killing such instincts from childhood. When we are born, we are whole with everything intact. Like a butcher we start fragmenting ourselves and others. Some parts are valued, others are not.

It takes a lifetime for us to go back to our natural selves. We have no idea who am I and who are you. We attend training programmes, Sufi teachings and thousands of processes to reignite our spontaneity, our truth.

What a tragedy!

# 34

# MEMORIES FLOOD MY BEING

Thinking about significant moments that shifted my life has been a challenge.

Memories flood my being. I feel overwhelmed at one level; at another level I can clearly see my patterns.

I was born into a large family, being the fifth child among the six siblings. An avid reader, I would read anything that I could lay my hands on. I read famous authors both in English and Hindi literature. That started forming my identity. Scarlett O'Hara from *Gone with the Wind* had a tremendous impact on me. Ayn Rand, Kafka, Camus, Charles Dickens, all left an everlasting impact.

Romantic poetry uplifted me. Just to give you a little flavour.

# 35

# NURTURE THE CHILD IN YOU

In a recent programme, people kept asking me my age. They were surprised by my energy and passion, I guess. Some said they see me as a role model, others really appreciated what I bring.

I started thinking and reflecting on what all this might mean – why is age the defining piece for a person?

We forgive people based on their age. S/he is too young to understand. We love people based on their age and give it some kind of title. You are like my sister, daughter, sister-in-law, mother, brother types. Playing safe, probably!?

We expect from people based on age. We tolerate nonsense based on age. Even when someone dies, the first question that's asked is how old was he or she. If one says ninety, then it's ok! Really?

We hire and fire people based on age, forgetting the uniqueness of people. If one asks someone what is unique about them, they say nothing. I am just an ordinary, average person.

We refuse to acknowledge the uniqueness of each individual. A ninety year old can beat a mighty thirty year old with her wit, energy and sense of humour.

This obsession with age is so limiting, creating rigid boundaries around our enthusiasm for life. People are reprimanded for not dressing according to their age. From where has such conditioning emerged? Our minds have been filled from a young age with these notions.

Thankfully, your uniqueness has nothing to do with age. It's all based on what you value in life, on the lens you are looking through. How open and curious are you? Love like there is no tomorrow and live like you have all the time in the world. Each sight, smell, touch creates a new understanding and you create a path as you go along.

Nurture the child in you which you are currently killing every day.

Cry, laugh, get angry, be sensuous. You will live long, I promise you.

# 36

# IT IS SO BLOODY SUBTLE!

Mirror, mirror on the wall
Who is the fairest of them all?

This need for someone else to tell us is the hole we get into.

Now this other person has power over you. It is so bloody subtle! Self-doubt is the killer. The shivering and trembling of lips waylays us and diverts us from our path. Really.

Even when the whole world praises you at your deepest level you don't believe. At some level this becomes a defence mechanism, mostly against ourselves. Taking risks, taking the initiative is so risky. Staying within the four walls of our world spells safety.

So much of our passion and potential is sacrificed at this altar. Self-doubt is a disease that keeps stealthily spreading like a cancer. It's almost self-denial. The other sibling of this is the need to prove ourselves to the world, and above all to ourselves. The need to add value keeps us silent most of the time till we find a way to strike.

We believe this is our secret weapon, a way to wield power, not realising that it's draining our power, making us dependent on the approval of others. When I can't appreciate myself, how can I extend that to others? We build a great narrative around ourselves and tell ourselves stories about why we should play safe, yet hanker after recognition.

Our inner world plays havoc with our dreams, our shadow overshadows everything and the beauty is we remain happily unaware.

# 37

# NOT ENOUGH

The age-old myth seems to be that only competition and comparison bring out the best in people. So, right from childhood, you are compared with your siblings and the neighbours' children. You are fed on stories of your cousins who accomplished so much or were so docile, who never talked back to their parents. Basically, everybody was goodness personified compared to you. Recall all such instances when even teachers compared you with an older sibling or the best student. Not only in terms of behaviour, skills or intelligence, but also physical beauty, which was the worst of all, especially for girls. From skin colour to length of hair, to facial features and height.

I remember when I had just entered college one so-called well-wisher aunt had come over. Looking at me she said 'she is pretty but so short'. This 'but' business was killing me. I remember retorting back to her that there is more beauty and advantages in being short. You are not very tall yourself. My mom glared at me and I got a big lecture later from her. Why wasn't that woman given a lecture? I wondered.

This is what gives birth to powerlessness, a sense of insecurity, a lack of confidence and an inability to take compliments.

How many of us have grown up with this kind of rubbish! The need for approval and acceptance from the external world rules our lives. While the real issue is that we are not able to accept ourselves as we are. It feels so sad growing up with comparisons and competition instead of experiencing love just for being who we are.

We are made to lose who we are, and then keep running to find it. Who am I really? We attend many programmes to discover who we really are, below the layers and layers of rubbish that we have accumulated over years. It is such a self-defeating battle.

I would rate the race for competing and comparison as the most harmful in the journey of life. So we suppress our feelings and shift from being to doing. Forgetting the joys of adventure and discovery. Abandoning that child somewhere in this seductive world of 'not enough'!

## 38

# LOVE LIKE THERE IS
# NO TOMORROW

There are many survivors of COVID. Some of the stories are so touching – of bravery and positivity. Some bring tears as some young and old people have passed on.

There is no other lesson that's more important than being in the present – take one day at a time. Love like there is no tomorrow, dance like this is the moment.

Wishing everyone long life and stay safe.

# 39

# THAT WAS WRITTEN IN ONE BREATH!

What is stirring me just now is a note I received from a colleague appreciating my work in the lab. When colleagues reach out with an open heart it fills the soul to the brim. It's not restricted to one or two lines but a full expression of the heart and soul, so genuinely stated that it brings tears to the eyes.

How often do we take the time to express ourselves so completely in our appreciation of another person? There is a kind of stinginess in our expression as if by being in the flow we are undercutting ourselves. It is only a person who is centred in herself and has superb confidence who can let praise be expressed whole-heartedly. So much so that it stirs the soul of the receiver. It is full of respect for self and the other. It talks of generosity and builds intimacy.

Why don't we want to go all out to embrace the appreciative part of ourselves? It only adds to our growth and the receiver's growth. It speaks volumes about the giver and in the bargain the receiver recognises the impact it had on her.

This genuine, whole-hearted praise can activate a healthy environment where there is a celebration of expression. We talk of competence. This is one competence that we should strive to have as it has numerous benefits at the intra-, inter- and group levels. It acts as adrenalin racing in the bloodstream.

A word of caution. If it becomes a gimmick then it had better stay dormant. The key is genuineness and not holding back. It's not being extravagant. But really describing in detail what touched you and the impact it had on you fully.

It's like the dark clouds gathering, then bringing down rain on a hot summer day.

# 40

# WHAT AM I GIVING BIRTH TO IN THE MOMENT?

Today we are being asked by the feminine aspect of creation to live according to the rhythms and cycles of nature.

There is a time to be active and there is a time to be still.

Reconnecting with our natural rhythms and honouring our inner wisdom will help us to live in harmony with Mother Earth.

If we want to continue life on Earth, what is it we are being asked to nurture, to heal and to transform?

What am I giving birth to in the moment?

# 41

# JUST TRY IT

Being in the here and now is a tough process. It's not easy or simple to follow. Our stories keep us on track, holding on to what happened long ago, a few months or weeks back. Even yesterday is more prominent than today. Our inner world is enmeshed with this. Our mind keeps wandering and we are not in touch with what's going on in the moment. How our feelings are being generated and how they keep knocking on our door. We do not respond to this knock.

The past is so much more significant and the inner critic is helping in keeping the moments out. We have lost our awareness and consciousness about the field of the present moment. If not the past, then the future is creating more anxiety.

I remember when a friend of mine had fallen in love. Her parents kept pushing her about whether he would eventually marry her. This burden and anxiety got to the young couple. Their free-flowing moments went for a toss. And finally they broke off. The romance went out of the window.

Most of us are guilty of killing the present moments with future anxiety. We don't go with the flow and soak in all the sensations fully. While being out with friends, our heart is beating with anxiety for the next day, or the remnants of the past keep interrupting till we stop enjoying it. Under the effects of alcohol we can forget about everything. We then play truant.

Make an effort to know what sensations are happening in your body, what you are feeling and what the impact is on you. Sharing that can lead to unimaginable intimacy. The joy is real, the tears are not fake.

## 42

# I AM PICKING UP THE SMALL CHANGES

As I am becoming a regular walker, I have started to recognise the pigeons and crows. I miss them when I don't see them. They also don't fly away on seeing me. They disregard me and go on doing whatever they are immersed in. To me, this spells trust that I won't harm them. The yellow gulmohars were in full bloom a week back. Now they are losing most of their flowers, instead the red gulmohars are blossoming. I am picking up small changes as they are happening. Beautiful *ehsaas*, realisation.

The group was flowing. Till the end they were disagreeing with each other and expressing themselves fully. What a powerful group it had become! Not hesitating to add their truth and feelings. Each one had shifted. They were facilitating themselves and doing a great job. When we were designing the closure, my co-facilitator and I came up with a design. As we were freezing the design, a thought struck me to ask them to design their own closure. Lo and behold, to our great delight and surprise they created the same design we were thinking about. What synchronicity!

# 43

# POWER IS A DYNAMIC PROCESS

This is a story about how we give up our power. Waiting for our turn to speak, expecting someone else to rescue us then wondering why people don't listen to us. My voice is not heard. They have their gang and only the favourite ones get heard. I am invisible. I share something but it seems to have no impact. Almost the same opinion expressed by someone else grabs attention. I lose confidence then. I withdraw and don't feel like contributing anymore. What's wrong with me, please tell me. I just can't communicate properly. I end up explaining a lot. Why did I say what I said, what was my intention?

Nothing seems to have any impact.

I feel so sick. I am not going to show my emotions anymore. I smile a lot when I am in turmoil inside. I want to disconnect from my feelings and remain my logical self. Anyways, nobody understands me. I can't make any more efforts.

So on and so forth. Does this sound familiar?

I am so scared of making mistakes, I think a lot before I venture forth. I want to look competent and in control. I may be dying a hundred times a day but put up a brave front. I want to project a very strong image. My inner world cannot peep through under any circumstances. I can't let my vulnerability show. I can manage and shoulder all responsibilities. My hurts and disappointments are mine to deal with. I don't need help. I am an independent, capable and confident person.

This is how we give up our power and start creating irrational beliefs. The stories we tell ourselves. Very Bollywood style, replete with villains, hero, heroine and sidekicks. I didn't know that my power lies in the way my eyes confront yours, the way my body arches forward, my booming voice, my uniqueness, my ability to feel, think and, above all, care. My listening and observing, my authenticity, playfulness and ability to be light-hearted and intense.

Who holds the power? Nobody can steal your power if you become aware of how you have been giving it up, and instead reclaim your power.

## 44

# WHERE ARE WE HEADED?

Coaching is the greatest gift. I wish teachers would also learn coaching and draw learning from children rather than pushing. Instead of shrinking the kids, expand them.

Nature is playing havoc. When will we wake up to mindless development? We are just exploiting the earth and not giving back anything. Our ancestors and natives knew better. With all our education and knowledge where are we heading? Lamenting big time. Good morning...

Curiosity gets blamed. It was the thing that killed the cat. We refrain from curiosity. What a great loss to humanity. What are you curious about?

The feminine perspective is as important to any decision making as other perspectives. That's when a picture becomes complete. An awareness that the feminine perspective is different. Let's not desexualise ourselves for the acceptance and approval bit. Life will be a rainbow when all perspectives are included.

Emotion is our response to life. Feelings are our essence. When one feels deeply, one connects with self and others in a way that leaves a mark.

# 45

# DISCOVERING NEW NOTES

When I express myself, my space expands and the freedom creates more space for life.

The flow of emotions is like the flow of a river.
It has a purpose and destination.
The less one tries to understand it, the better for the river.

Joy lies in connecting with self. Like singing from the gut level, not just from the throat, and discovering new notes.

Being vulnerable is not a choice. It's a reality of living. What we do with that vulnerability can either open doors to deeper connection or throw up walls that stifle growth.

Vulnerability is more than an ability and competence. It is a potent source of power. A way to reclaim your power!

# 46

# LIKE BEGGARS WE KEEP STANDING

Who is a maverick? How do we define a maverick? The dictionary definition is a person who does not behave or think like everyone else, but has independent, unusual opinions.

Why are these traits suppressed and why do we want people to follow set rules and paths, despite history having been witness to millions of innovations by such people? It's a great tragedy. How many of us are trapped for most of our lives in this prison of acceptance, approval, validation? The fears are triggered whenever we want to take the unusual route, unexplored and unfamiliar. Well-wishers feed these fears under the garb of concern and love.

So many talents remain dormant under the tyranny of the known and tested paths. Like beggars we keep standing with a begging bowl for validation, disempowering ourselves and giving authority to the so-called well-wishers to continue their rule over us. We have lost our power to think and experiment.

It's a kind of drama being enacted on a regular basis. Sometimes we are aware but hold back such emotions. There is no problem in looking for validation, but be upfront about it. Ask for validation, experience comfort in rejection.

We can't have our cake and eat it too. Interestingly, the other party knows their hold over you. It is in their interest to continue this facade of concern and love while continuing to demand their pound of flesh.

# 47

# VOLUNTARISM AS A VALUE

I find that this is the highest value and creates a sense of ownership and commitment. Inherent in it is taking initiative and passion. It calls for freedom and making choices in freedom. Deep democracy thrives on this value. There is no pressure and no force applied.

I belong to two organisations where you become part of them because that's what you desire and because of the rigour you need to put in to earn the membership. You give back to the organisation because that's where you grew and learnt. Voluntarily taking on roles and contributing because you align with the purposes of the organisation.

The two such organisations that I became part of are ISABS and NTL Institute for Applied Behavioral Sciences. I have experienced successful consultants being part of them, offering their services voluntarily, committing time, energy, effort and above all passion.

I was just wondering why commercial organisations do not have this value as the backbone of their workplace. This particular value values me as an individual and safeguards my sense of freedom. The creativity bubbles in me and I feel safe to experiment. That doesn't mean that there won't be politics – it's not utopia.

But when we talk of inclusion and diversity, people include themselves of their own volition bringing their diversity.

I would love to hear your views.

# 48

# IT IS TIME TO CLAIM OUR REAL POWER

How we misunderstand feminine and masculine energy and behaviours, above all marginalising some energies as they are disapproved of by our culture, society, parents and corporates. We talk a lot about diversity and inclusion but excel in exclusion. We haven't even bothered to go deep into the subject to understand fully these concepts and how we have grown. What kind of biases do we carry?

Crying is for girls, strong boys don't cry, don't be a girl; you are a girl, remember that!

As grown-ups, we don't even understand how we have felt abandoned by our own mother or father, and advised not to feel.

Be practical. Success is being measured by a lack of feelings.

What is our connection with mother earth? With nature? Only to use it for our pleasure?

It is time to claim our real power. Shiva's *Ardhanareeshvara* (the half male, half female god) that we worship, without understanding what is being offered to us. It's time to call the shots and not gravitate only to what has been taught to us.

Let's use our own thinking, discernment, understanding, and deep dive into our native wisdom. Stop being the sheep to be led by these forces. Religion, caste, class, tradition and so on. '*Mazhab nahin sikhata aapas mein bair karna.*' Religions do not teach us to fight or create differences against each other.

Happy seeding new thoughts and feelings for future generations. What's the legacy we want to leave behind?

# 49

# HAPPY JOURNEY

Just sitting on the porch and watching the sky, as clouds gathered and lightning happened, almost putting on a show for us. The silence was so provocative. The process looked as if the clouds were clapping together and lightning was being generated. Simply awesome...

Holding back is quite a phenomenon in our lives. We hold back words, our spontaneity, actions, tears, laughter, anger, sadness, our urges, loves, joys, struggles, confusion, jealousy, et cetera. Fundamentally, everything about ourselves.

The metaphor that comes to mind is the kitchen sink. Holding back results in getting stuck and the water starts to overflow. Sometimes we hold back our breath just to let the moment pass. Relationships become transactional and just over the surface. Holding back is against the flow of life. Survival becomes the ultimate goal. Anyhow, somehow, howsoever.

Holding back as it may not be understood. Let the

moment pass. Holding on to memories, especially the negative moments, and judging each new event through that lens is a self-defeating process.

The tears are forever threatening to roll down like those of a spoilt brat. Not listening to your heartbeats. We hide them, yet still they escape your vigilant hold. Showing up is growing. The tears of joy and of sadness both transform us.

Last night an intimate session among three of us as colleagues, as friends took us into a deep adventure of discovery of self and others. A deep connection got formed. Genuineness and emotions took us on a ride that's rare in this hectic life. There was no holding back, just a flow, like many rivers having a *sangam*, a union as they move towards the ocean, the final destination of depth and pearls where waves carry you to another world, unknown and exciting.

# 50

# DISCOVERY OF SELF

What is this fear of being judged? Where does it come from? Look how it cripples our lives. The fact remains that everyone judges everyone, including the ones who have fear. It intrigues me.

People weigh each word they speak and hardly open their mouths, censoring a thousand times what they should say or not. Holding back their perspectives and diverse views. One benefit is that you develop a rich imagination, making all kinds of assumptions about others. Or you speak only when you are adding value, hence diminishing other people. It's a strange game, creating illusions about oneself, sounding like an expert but with shallow knowledge.

This life becomes a constant struggle. One of the needs behind it is the desire to be liked by all. So that people don't think ill of the person. This is a killer. That constant, mostly fake smile on the face, the taking care of others' feelings all the time, the inability to say no.

This is not even an awareness of others' feelings. It is all about assumptions. S/he will be hurt and feel bad. So we are trying to please all kinds of people just to be liked by them.

It's a crazy game. Imagining other people to be so fragile and oneself to be superhuman. You end up treating people as incapable.

I read a book called *Will The Real Me Please Stand Up?* I loved the title. The real me is on a vacation most of the time. The fact is that everybody loves people who are so sweet and polite, people who would never confront. I wonder at times what kind of inner world would that be.

The choice is really ours and the consequences too. Are you going to hold your whole life to ransom? What part of you is being disowned by you which you are afraid to show? What parts of you are acceptable to you? I feel sad. It is so much easier to develop and grow yourself rather than hide behind a smile. Try to add value by just being you. It's a long journey, I agree, but worth taking. Will the real you please stand up?

## 51

# FEELINGS

Lab after lab, the only difficulty people have is to get in touch with their feelings. To locate their feelings and to express them. We don't even understand the difference between feeling and thinking. What kind of disability is that?

This is uprooting the self and our soul. We have been brainwashed into thinking. As if thinking is the only asset we can have. While the most important decisions are taken from the heart… that passion which drives us crazy. The most satisfying moments come when we feel touched in unprecedented ways. Sadness and depression have led to the creation of significant works, whichever field you look at. That overwhelming gut feeling that leads you to unknown paths.

Anger pulsating which motivated you to push your boundaries and react from basic humaneness. It can be stormy and dysfunctional yet nothing gets accomplished until this emotion gets aroused and you are moved to move.

Love carries a bad reputation. That's the time when everything is in sync. You feel like an astrologer, intuitively experiencing and being able to sense. Be it a child, a lover, a parent, nature, hobbies, a project, a friend. Love is devastating yet creative. You are so alive to poetry, songs, colours, rain, lightning, snow and water.

Fear is such an integral part of our growing up. What's the point in denying it and acting fearless? Courage comes from fear. If we don't feel fear we can't experience the courage of standing up.

I remember as a college student going up on stage to recite a poem or for a debate. My stomach would churn, go in hundreds of waves, making me more nervous. As I would climb on stage some devil would catch hold of me and I would be my audacious self. The more scared I was, the better job I did. Not to let myself down. That creative tension was inspiring.

## 52

# LIFE WILL EXPAND

I am sure all of us have experienced these emotions. When you flow from your passion, you feel you have stepped on some live wire sending shockwaves across, bringing out the brilliance.

Even what we think is ultimately accompanied by intense emotions. The more we realise that thinking is tame and feelings alone can just be wild, the better it is for life. Why do we cry when someone dies, leaves us, abandons us? Why do we laugh when happy news hits us?

Think it over, explore the umpteen moments when you gave your best.

Let's connect with our feelings and express them. Life will expand. There is something happening to me as I write. So many emotions are stirred.

I am so glad.
I feel more energy.

Share something that triggered you on reading it.

# 53

# INTERPERSONAL WETLANDS

Interpersonal space between two people is a sacred space created for experimentation, seeding new ideas and the messiness that ensues. With the right manure, enough water and care, these spaces can become rich – or they can just be wetlands inviting the inevitable.

I used to love the quote 'walk with me in mud, my friend' and used it as my tag line for emails and everything. Walking in mud as a metaphor is an invitation to have the freedom to be messy, dirty and even ugly sometimes. Together we can take more risk. If I am afraid of getting dishevelled, then I will walk only on pristine paths. No adventure and fun will await me. With a kindred soul we are not afraid of the unknown, catching those snails by their tails.

Have you ever caught yourself rolling around with laughter after making a silly mistake with a friend? How many times do you do that at your workplace?

What is intimacy if you cannot see into me? Interpersonal space can open new vistas, like Alice in Wonderland. Most conflicts get created in that space, seeming threatening like a roaring tiger. But the making up has all the stars coming out in their finery, glittering on a dark night.

Why are we so scared of our authentic self? As if like a truant child it will cause you embarrassment. Yes, embarrassment acts like a defence to newness, that tender green leaf that's just getting born. What is embarrassing about enjoying the mud, lying down in it and throwing mud at each other, resulting in that messy hug?

I read the book *Interpersonal Underworld* by William Shultz. I loved the title. There is much happening on the surface but 80 per cent is underworld. Our fears, needs, desires, ambitions, secrets, unconsciousness, pasts, dreams, expectations and so on.

They are adding unnecessary mess to everything we set out to cook. It's like two worlds colliding and a silent challenge to quieten the inner critic who keeps reminding us to play safe.

What does the mud remind you of? I once slipped on a rain-drenched road and landed on a heap of mud. After the initial shock of spoiling my clothes, I went with the flow and danced in the rain, enjoying every bit of the moment. I could have got angry with myself or cursed the rain, the slippery road or my shoes. Millions of things to blame for such a catastrophe added more to the muddy waters. I saw it as an opportunity knocking at my door to have a new experience.

We can rave and rant about another person but share with them all the devils that are a part of our psyche and theirs. Does the space between the two of us expand or shrink?

Creating intimacy needs real alcohol mixed in our being, no fake stuff. A great cocktail requires stirring up and shaking to get the authentic flavour of life. Experience the joy of headiness with innovation to boot, in that fertile ground of interpersonal space.

Happy hunting!

# 54

# A QUESTION OF QUESTIONS

What do I want to do now that my role has been cut off? Just like a branch is cut off from a tree. I don't have the job anymore. I am very sad at one level, but at another it's a relief to be free again. I never liked what I was doing. Good riddance!?

After a couple of months, I don't know where I am heading. I am not sure what I want to do. Another job isn't my cup of tea. But I need to earn and do something creative, have time for my interests, go trekking, et cetera. But I really feel like a failure at one level. I make great plans for doing something but that fizzles out soon. I am back to my dilemmas.

What is attractive about life? What grabs you really? That's the issue. So many things, but I don't know what really grabs me. What's the value that brings out your passion?

Freedom is what I want, the freedom to do all that my heart takes a fancy to. You know, to create something.

I wonder, am I procrastinating? Just whiling away my time? I love meeting people and having conversations. The rest of the things suck my energy. I feel shrunk.

What are you avoiding?

Hmmm, maybe failure. I have a fear of failure, you know, probably that blocks me and I keep dilly dallying. Yeah, that's it – and I need power.

This doesn't let me attempt anything. Taking a risk is a big step. What's the risk you are talking about?

Tell me more, like if I try something and really fail, I can't face myself. I need approval from so many people. What will they think of me? At one level, I don't care but deep down it matters a lot. I act as if I couldn't care less, but my god it hurts in my guts.

How about working with failure? Failing is always a great possibility. It can be fun to fail and try something else or more. What do you think? How does this grab you?

I am feeling a new energy coming in. I never thought about it like that. I want to create possibilities of failing and enjoying the process. Questions are a very interesting process. 'Raising questions', 'asking questions' and 'questioning' have very different connotations. Questions that empower us or disempower us. Questions with raised eyebrows or questions with a lopsided smile. Questions that elevate us or pull us down. Questions that are meant to humiliate us or genuine questions seeking information. Provocative or sarcastic.

They represent caste, class or gender, spelling authority or humility. Creating humour, fun or simply playing the fool. Discriminating or collaborative. They could be close-ended, demanding one kind of response, or open-ended, letting you swim around. Secretive, selective, political or psychological. Full of rage or sadness. There are also happy, innocent questions.

As I started to write I didn't realise there could be so many types of categories. Questions that are a veiled threat or teasing questions. Flirting with you, loving you, pulling your leg types. Caring questions, caressing ones coming straight from the heart and overwhelming you. Romantic questions and sexy ones that leave your sensations to take you beyond the skies.

Then there are those that manipulate you and emotionally blackmail you. Questions that floor you, make you think and reflect. Those that push you out of your comfort zone, stretch your boundaries. Questions that make you learn and unlearn, creating new paths. Or even the questions that come from our ignorance, expressing our vulnerability. The questions that spell strength and make you dive deeper. Rapid ones and slow ones. Questions that serve you or divert you from the real task. Those tiny ones that leave a lingering doubt about your ability or beauty. Half said ones that leave a long pause. Questions that take you to the dark spaces of your past, and then those ones that make you wonder about life.

Perennial questions like who am I and what's my purpose on this earth? The best part is that most of them don't necessarily warrant answers. Many questions about profit and loss, practical stuff and so on. I have left them for the time being. But why have I left them?

Question and claim your power!

## 55

# CONNECTING IS A DEEP PROCESS

There are always stories in stories. Each one's story of the same incident is different. Listening without defence may be the only route to understanding without compromising your story. The possibility of holding all the stories together, a way of creating the whole story. All the parts are critical.

Have we forgotten the art of connecting with people in a manner that's satisfying? Or is it all about task? As long as that's being fulfilled, I don't need to know who you are, what makes your heart sing or why you all of a sudden become tearful. What matters to you and what matters to me, and how does it matter? Let's get on with life. Who has the time? We have fun forwarding messages on WhatsApp or sharing a beer together.

While I was having lunch with a friend who I hadn't seen for a long time, I noticed some sadness in her eyes, in the way she mentioned her son. Out of concern and curiosity I asked 'what about your husband?' She shared that she was no longer with him, having walked out of their long marriage a year ago. We had such a wonderful conversation about ourselves. We connected deeply. I suddenly came to know her more. I am sure all of us often notice and pick up on something but avoid pushing the unwritten boundaries. We feel lonely so many times, yearning to pour our heart out to someone who will understand.

Trusting ourselves and others is a big risk. Will I be understood or accepted? Why open up when finally I have to deal with it. I am not just talking about problems, but a conversation that makes us connect with self and others.

Trust is the main ingredient. There are plenty of messages we have included, inherited and internalised. Don't trust, keep your problems to yourself, who has the time to listen to you? Be self-sufficient, independent, meet everyone with a smile. Fundamentally, you don't know anything. Trust me, you are too naive.

This goes on dictating our lives. Human resources. So we use each other for our own purposes. As soon as the outcome is achieved we forget and move on to others.

Connecting is a deep process. Each encounter can be enriching, creating memories and learning for all. But are you willing to invest? In adventure, discoveries and noticing. So that working together, enjoying together or discussing can be such beautiful experiences.

## 56

# HAPPY LEARNING

Learning is a lifelong journey. We are always learning something from our day-to-day lives, millions of encounters, reading and above all, our mistakes. Things like I vow never to do this again, will never give my heart away, et cetera. How much do we learn from our achievements and successes? What part of us made that happen? That's where the real growth lies – in creating time to critically examine the high points in our lives.

You will find that each one of us has certain patterns that help us overcome. I was listening to a friend yesterday over lunch. She recently walked out of her marriage. Her courage to face life on her own stood out for me. Her valuing her own independence marked who she is. She was looking so much more glamorous, which was her inner beauty oozing out.

Learning to unlearn is a huge step forward. How do you really learn? Is it a deliberate act or something thrust on you? With the recent example of the slapping at the Oscars, I learnt how lots of people were becoming oppressors themselves while taking one side or the other. That moment needed compassion from all of us.

This binary approach to wrong and right doesn't help us to learn holistically. Learning cognitively is easier than experientially.

Creating spaces in our hearts and minds so that new images create new reflection and experiences.

Each moment has something tangible and intangible in it.

## 57

# FEARS ARE A PART OF LIFE

Leading with blocks that are always chasing you – like fear of failure or rejection, to name a few – is an uphill task. They are the architects of a leadership profile. When we don't pay attention to these, it leads to excessive control, micromanaging, undermining others' capabilities and so on. Such leaders can also be more worried about others' reactions to them. Their need for acceptance, approval, being liked plays havoc with them. We can lose the real purpose and meander into sweet nothings. The fears are mysterious partners taking decisions on our behalf.

We seem to become powerless. The intention and impact of our behaviour are very different. In a wildly spiralling world we are like lost babies playing with our favourite toys while new opportunities are knocking at the door. The known path and styles are preferred over experimentation. The need for safety is the fulcrum we revolve around. Taking risks with new awareness is like stepping into a minefield. In this confusion, we bank upon the tried and tested approaches.

These fears are real, no doubt. Leaning in to deal with them with full awareness is the new capability. Blades of grass bend with the wind and stay solidly entrenched. Their flexibility is the edge they have over solid trees that get uprooted in a storm.

Fears are a part of life. All kinds of fears can stop our growth and we can remain unaware of the source of the infection. Treating this malady with antibiotics won't help. Awareness, action and taking responsibility are the dose that helps fight the infection. It does not mean that you can become free of fears. They are a part of us. A lack of acknowledgement and vulnerability creates more damage. I can skirt around my fears but they grab me at the unlikeliest moments so stealthily and surreptitiously that I surrender. In my heart I know what I am doing and not doing. That's my undoing.

# 58

# SOME FOOD FOR THOUGHT

Adaptability and resilience are the two words doing the rounds these days. What are they asking us to be? Fundamentally to remain open and respond in the here and now. To use our discerning sense and shift our perspective instead of getting stuck in planning and rigid stances. To be like the river and flow, creating a new path and opportunities wherever there are boulders in the way. Nothing can be permanent. Transience is life. It's all about the here and now, to flow with constant change. The sheer joy of it.

Like seasons change and everything changes according to the seasons. We change clothes according to the season, so why not our attitudes and perspectives as the situation demands? Instead of reacting, why not respond and move forward, to rise from below? Even a dead tree dares to sprout new leaves and branches after being dead for a while.

Why not us human beings? Why are we stuck in so-called traditions and conditioning when conditions and circumstances have changed?

## 59

# BE THE FLOWING RIVER THAT BRINGS CALM

Relationship coaching is about your presence, your authentic behaviour and how you create the container for deep dialogue to emerge. For differences to be articulated in a caring way without fear. The deep trust in the process and the joy of exploring and discovering parts of us we had previously marginalised. The only facilitation I do between two people comes from my trust in the here and now. Go with the flow and share observations. I have no need for attention or contributions.

Be the flowing river that brings calm and space to reflect.

# 60

# CREATING NEW POSSIBILITIES

Nature is very deep. It is not just the outer beauty that's captivating. Take a pause and dive into its complexity; new vistas open up.

Tragedies happen.

The art lies in our response. It spells our essence and our values. In a crisis, our values and our integrity shine through.

We can shout and scream about revenge and power. Hatred with hatred has never won anything. It is a downward spiral. Love and compassion are the key ingredients. Right and timely decisions to support what we believe in and actions that speak louder than rhetoric.

Creating space for exploration and discovery depends entirely on who you are as a person, your own flow impacts the participants. That streak of fun, non-judgement, curiosity and childlike wisdom conveys and touches the hearts of the others deeply. Stirring a new rhythm, almost musical in nature with resonance.

My anxiety creates another flow of nature, it's jumping, hesitant, bumping over even small stones, imagining gaps and creating stress as it pushes its way through.

So watch out for what's alive in you.

My own sense of freedom becomes the wind of change for others. My energy and love create new possibilities.

What do you say?

## 61

# A MIRACLE IS ON ITS WAY

Creating new possibilities needs deep work with self. Our mind is stuck with beliefs that no longer serve us. We are satisfied with two or three options. It's an interesting phenomenon. I discovered my fluidity as I was playing the game *Words of Wonders*. It is difficult to create words with limited letters. Something that's right in front of your eyes, you can't see. Suddenly a light is turned on and you realise it was there all along. The more you push yourself, the more possibilities emerge. It's hard, and so much easier to be comfortable and give up.

Giving up is an option too.

Allow the artist in you to try more colours, mixing them, creating new shades, and you will have an array of shining new colours to paint a beautiful picture.

Shake yourself and you will find ideas scattered

around you. At the dining table, its legs on the carpet, in the pictures that are hanging, so on and so forth.

Nature is full of possibilities, new thoughts conjure new images. A miracle is on its way, knocking on your window.

Just open the window, a new wind will blow you away. Sunrays will play with the child in you. Stop being practical and be a horse that flies, like the little prince tending his roses.

# A FOUR-LETTER WORD

My whole being is shaken
Blood rushing to my face
Each pore of being is alive as it were
Each part is vibrating
The feeling of every pore receiving the blood supply and waking up
To a new day
The feelings that I am accosting are being held by so many hands
Cajoling me like a child
I have no misgivings about being dropped and breaking my head
It's the heart that is beating so fast and keeping me buoyant
Floating despite the high tide
Love can weave new fabric with so many threads and colours
Each pore of my being is open
And vibrating like hell
It's a four-letter word
Written across my being
L. O. V. E.

# 63

# WHAT THE HELL ARE FEELINGS?

Stop feeling so much, be practical and logical. You will not succeed if you feel everything. Get on with life. These are some common tips for success. How many of us have not been told this mantra and been chided for being emotional? I have always wondered about it. Will I exist if I stop feeling?

Beautiful, brilliant sunshine brings me such joy, rains shower me with so many emotions. A young boy persuading me to buy flowers when I was travelling. His desperation brought tears to my eyes. I don't enjoy watching a film if it doesn't move me emotionally. The sudden appearance of a loved one changes my mood. Somebody giving me a compliment in a very genuine way transforms my heartbeat. My favourite team winning makes me shriek with joy, has me jumping. Love brings tears, changes my rhythm of life. A sudden look of sadness helps me to be curious about you. The futility and boredom of a meeting help me to realise that something is drastically wrong. Disappointment, envy, jealousy get me in touch with my deeper self. I wake up in the morning because my creative imagination is an alarm for me.

Anger is the most potent of all emotions. When I lose this capacity, it's indifference and apathy all around me. I feel angry at so many things that are going around nowadays, at the war that is devastating Ukraine, Gaza and its people. How caste, colour, religion are dominating our humanness. Millions of things that are unfair. What's the net result? We have become insensitive to social issues, the environment. The earth is suffocating with plastic, birds and animals are dying. The immune system is at its lowest. Most people don't feel passionately enough, hence apathy sets in.

What's the price we are ready to pay for fragmenting ourselves? We are not noticing little things that happen around us. Appreciating is a feeling after all, spontaneity has gone on vacation.

Feelings are a natural resource that we all have from childhood just like other natural resources – forests, rivers, mountains. It's all dried up. In our enthusiasm to climb the ladder of success we have embraced logic alone. How illogical is that! People have feelings: understanding this and responding constitute the greatest asset for a leader. Yet we are all filled and conditioned with homilies of boys don't cry, don't be emotional, keep your feelings at home and so on.

Another game is to feel but don't express and share. Keep guessing.

As I am writing I feel anger rising in me at the stupidity of all this conditioning. Yet when a baby smiles, laughs, cries, loves us even without words, how elated we feel. We know deep down in our heart it is normal. What an irony!

Now I am feeling exhausted. There is still so much more I want to say, probably part two will follow.

# 64

# IT JUST CUT MY HEART INTO PIECES

Social distancing will be extended by fifteen days, maybe more. While some people are thinking and dreaming of going out, I am wondering about those people who have lost their earnings. Restarting work.

I've heard about one organisation that is laying off 2,000 people. I am sure that's the story of many so-called humane organisations.

I shudder to think about millions of such people. One day when we made a different menu and we were enjoying it, my helper said: 'you seem to be celebrating when so many people in my village have nothing to eat.'

It just cut my heart into pieces.

Although he is among the fortunate ones yet his heart was with others like him.

Extraordinary times need a different treatment.

Let's hope we all come out of it being richer in soul and with the attitude to be holistic.

•

# 65

# THE LEADER IS READY TO FLOW

Awareness, according to me, is the biggest piece in any leadership journey. What do we understand about it? There are so many dimensions of it. Discovering my needs, values, fears, anxieties, my insecurities, my dreams, my passion, my purpose in life, my joys, sorrows, love, the fun part of me, my story, my shadow, and on and on.

It doesn't end with awareness; that's where it begins. The next step is exploration: questions starting with 'when', 'what', 'how' or 'where' help to discover our deep-rooted stuff, along with the pearls and shadows.

Exploration leaves us surprised and delighted, at times shocked. Enhancing our quest for more, we don't hesitate to go into the dark corners of our being, opening doors which were invisible to the naked eye. Like a curious child wanting more.

The third step is acknowledging and opening to our

long-lost friends. Leading with that knowledge of wholeness, we connect with ourselves, others and the environment. Empowering the self empowers others too. We can hold hands and open up our feelings, judgements, biases, beliefs and vulnerability. The joy of pushing our boundaries and embracing challenges creates more energy.

With self-awareness, exploration, self-realisation and owning up, the leader is ready to flow!

# ABOUT THE AUTHOR

Sushma Sharma, born in Amritsar, India in 1947, is a well-established organisational-development consultant and leadership coach. She now lives in Mumbai with her husband Raji. This is her first book.

www.ingramcontent.com/pod-product-compliance
Lightning Source LLC
Chambersburg PA
CBHW061221070526
44584CB00029B/3922